Cook with C

Table of Contents

Introduction

Chapter 1: Healthy Eating

1.1 Superfoods
1.2 Plant-Based Diets
1.3 Low-Carb Diets

Chapter 2: Quick and Easy Meals

2.1 One-Pot Meals
2.2 Sheet Pan Dinners
2.3 Slow Cooker Meals

Chapter 3: Global Cuisines

3.1 Mexican Cuisine
3.2 Italian Cuisine
3.3 Asian Cuisine

Chapter 4: Desserts

4.1 No-Bake Desserts
4.2 Gluten-Free Desserts
4.3 Vegan Desserts

One last thing,,,

Introduction

Welcome to the ultimate cooking experience!

Welcome to Cook with Chris! This book is your guide to creating delicious and nutritious meals that will have your family and friends begging for more. With plenty of easy-to-follow recipes, you'll be able to create meals that are sure to become family favourites. From quick weeknight dinners to show-stopping desserts, you'll find something for everyone.

Chris has been cooking for over 20 years and has perfected the art of creating flavourful and healthy dishes. He has a passion for food and loves to share his knowledge with others. In this book, he shares his favourite recipes and tips for making the most of your ingredients. He also provides helpful advice on how to make the most of your time in the kitchen and how to save money on groceries.

So, if you're looking for a way to make delicious meals with ease, then Cook with Chris is the perfect book for you. With easy-to-follow instructions and helpful tips, you'll be able to create meals that are sure to become family favourites. So, let's get cooking!

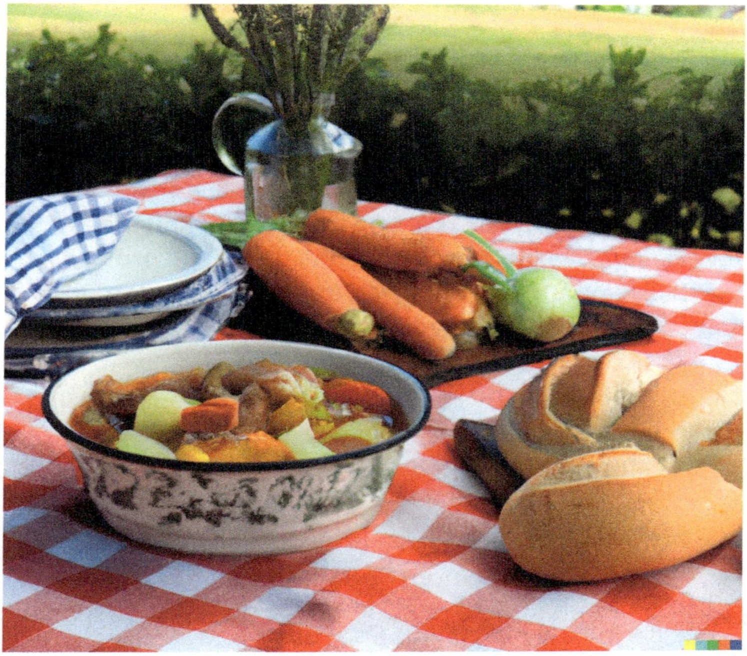

Chapter 1: Healthy Eating

1.1 Superfoods

Superfoods are like superheroes for your body! Packed with vitamins, minerals, and antioxidants, these nutrient-rich foods are essential for keeping your body healthy and strong. Superfoods can help boost your energy levels, improve your immunity, and even help protect against chronic diseases. So why not give your body the power it needs and add some superfoods to your diet today!

Here are some of the best superfoods to add to your diet:

- Avocados • Blueberries • Broccoli • Kale • Salmon • Walnuts

1.2 Plant-Based Diets

Plant-based diets are a great way to get all the essential nutrients your body needs while also being good for the environment. Eating a variety of plant-based foods can provide a wide range of vitamins, minerals, and antioxidants that can help protect against disease and promote overall health. Additionally, plant-based diets are typically lower in saturated fat and cholesterol, making them a healthier choice than diets that are high in animal-based foods.

Adding superfoods to your plant-based diet can be a great way to boost your nutrition and health. Superfoods are nutrient-dense foods that are packed with vitamins, minerals, antioxidants, and other beneficial compounds. Examples of superfoods include dark leafy greens, berries, nuts, seeds, and legumes. Eating these foods can help provide essential nutrients and help reduce your risk of chronic diseases. Plus, they can make your meals more flavorful and exciting. So, why not add some superfoods to your plant-based diet and reap the health benefits?

Over the next few pages are some delicious plant-based recipes to try:

Quinoa Salad with Roasted Vegetables

This Quinoa Salad with Roasted Vegetables is a great way to get in your daily servings of vegetables. The quinoa provides a great source of protein and fibre, while the roasted vegetables add a delicious flavour and texture. The combination of the quinoa and vegetables makes this dish a great source of vitamins, minerals, and antioxidants. Additionally, the healthy fats from the roasted vegetables help to keep you feeling full and satisfied. This dish is a great way to get in your daily servings of vegetables while also providing a healthy and delicious meal.

Ingredients:

- 1 cup of quinoa
- 2 cups of water
- 1 teaspoon of olive oil
- 1/2 teaspoon of salt
- 1/4 teaspoon of black pepper
- 1/2 teaspoon of garlic powder
- 1/4 teaspoon of cumin
- 1 red bell pepper, diced
- 1 zucchini, diced
- 1 yellow squash, diced
- 1/2 cup of cherry tomatoes, halved
- 1/4 cup of red onion, diced
- 1/4 cup of fresh parsley, chopped
- 1/4 cup of feta cheese, crumbled
- 1/4 cup of extra-virgin olive oil
- 2 tablespoons of freshly squeezed lemon juice
- 1 tablespoon of honey
- Salt and pepper to taste

Instructions:

1. Preheat the oven to 400°F.

2. In a medium saucepan, bring the quinoa and water to a boil. Reduce heat to low, cover, and simmer for 15 minutes or until the quinoa is tender.

3. Meanwhile, in a large bowl, combine the olive oil, salt, pepper, garlic powder, and cumin. Add the bell pepper, zucchini, squash, tomatoes, and onion to the bowl and toss to coat.

4. Spread the vegetables onto a baking sheet and roast in the preheated oven for 20 minutes or until the vegetables are tender.
5. In a small bowl, whisk together the olive oil, lemon juice, honey, salt, and pepper.

6. In a large bowl, combine the cooked quinoa, roasted vegetables, parsley, feta cheese, and dressing. Toss to combine.

7. Serve warm or cold. Enjoy!

Lentil Soup

Lentil soup is a delicious meal with many health benefits. Lentils are a great source of plant-based protein, fibre, and essential vitamins and minerals. They are also low in fat and calories, making them a great choice for weight loss and overall health. Lentils are also packed with antioxidants, which can help reduce inflammation and support a healthy immune system. Additionally, lentils are a great source of iron, which is important for energy production and red blood cell formation. Finally, lentils are a great source of complex carbohydrates, which can help keep you feeling full for longer and provide sustained energy throughout the day.

Ingredients:

- 1 tablespoon olive oil
- 1 onion, diced
- 2 cloves garlic, minced
- 2 carrots, diced
- 2 stalks celery, diced
- 1 teaspoon ground cumin
- 1 teaspoon ground coriander
- 1 teaspoon dried oregano
- 1 teaspoon smoked paprika
- 1/2 teaspoon ground turmeric
- 1/2 teaspoon ground black pepper
- 6 cups vegetable broth
- 2 cups dried green lentils, rinsed and drained
- 1 (14.5 ounce) can diced tomatoes
- 1 bay leaf
- 1/2 cup chopped fresh parsley
- Salt to taste

Instructions:

1. Heat the olive oil in a large pot over medium heat. Add the onion and garlic and cook until softened, about 5 minutes.

2. Add the carrots and celery and cook until softened, about 5 minutes.

3. Add the cumin, coriander, oregano, smoked paprika, turmeric, and black pepper and cook for 1 minute.

4. Add the vegetable broth, lentils, tomatoes, bay leaf, and parsley and bring to a boil.

5. Reduce the heat to low and simmer, covered, for 30 minutes or until the lentils are tender.

6. Remove the bay leaf and season with salt to taste.

7. Serve hot. Enjoy!

Veggie Burgers

Veggie burgers are a delicious and healthy alternative to traditional beef burgers. They are packed with plant-based proteins, vitamins, minerals, and fibre, making them a nutritious and filling meal. Veggie burgers are also a great way to get creative in the kitchen and can be customised to fit any dietary needs and preferences. Plus, they are a fun and tasty way to switch up your burger routine!

Ingredients:

- 1 cup cooked quinoa
- 1/2 cup cooked black beans
- 1/2 cup cooked lentils
- 1/2 cup cooked sweet potato
- 1/2 cup grated carrots
- 1/2 cup diced red onion
- 1/4 cup chopped fresh parsley
- 2 tablespoons olive oil
- 1 teaspoon garlic powder
- 1 teaspoon smoked paprika
- 1/2 teaspoon ground cumin
- 1/4 teaspoon salt
- 1/4 teaspoon black pepper
- 4 whole wheat buns

Instructions:

1. Preheat the oven to 375 degrees F.

2. In a large bowl, combine quinoa, black beans, lentils, sweet potato, carrots, red onion, and parsley.

3. In a small bowl, whisk together olive oil, garlic powder, smoked paprika, cumin, salt, and pepper.

4. Pour the oil mixture over the veggie mixture and stir until everything is evenly coated.

5. Form the mixture into 4 patties and place on a parchment-lined baking sheet.

6. Bake for 20-25 minutes, flipping halfway through.

7. Serve the veggie burgers on whole wheat buns with your favourite toppings. Enjoy!

Sweet Potato Fries

Sweet potato fries are a healthy option because they are a great source of vitamins, minerals, and dietary fibre. They are also low in calories and fat, making them a great choice for those looking to lose weight or maintain a healthy diet. Sweet potato fries also add a lot of colour and flavour to any plate of food. They are a great way to add a unique twist to traditional dishes, as well as a delicious side dish for any meal.

Ingredients:

- 2 large sweet potatoes
- 2 tablespoons olive oil
- 1 teaspoon garlic powder
- 1 teaspoon paprika
- 1 teaspoon dried oregano
- 1 teaspoon sea salt

Instructions:

1. Preheat the oven to 400 degrees F.

2. Peel and cut sweet potatoes into thin fry shapes.

3. Place sweet potato fries in a large bowl and drizzle with olive oil.

4. Add garlic powder, paprika, oregano, and sea salt and mix until all fries are evenly coated.

5. Spread sweet potato fries onto a baking sheet lined with parchment paper.

6. Bake for 20-25 minutes, flipping halfway through, until fries are golden brown and crispy.

7. Serve hot and enjoy!

1.3 Low-Carb Diets

Low-carb diets are popular for weight loss and health benefits because they help to reduce hunger and cravings, promote steady blood sugar levels, and reduce the risk of chronic diseases such as diabetes and heart disease. Low-carb diets also help to burn fat more efficiently and can help reduce the risk of obesity. Additionally, low-carb diets are often higher in protein and fibre, which can help to keep you feeling fuller for longer and help to reduce overall calorie intake.

Over the next few pages are some delicious low-carb recipes to try:

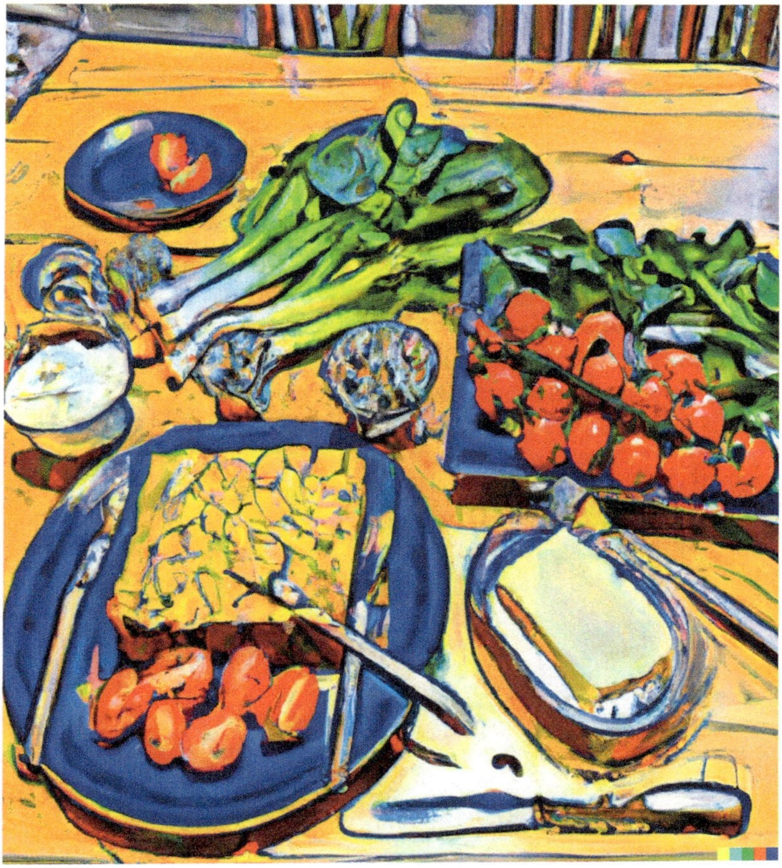

Zucchini Noodles with Pesto

Zucchini noodles with pesto are a healthy and delicious way to add flavour to any meal. Zucchini noodles are a low-carb and low-calorie alternative to traditional pasta, making them a great choice for those looking to lose weight or maintain a healthy lifestyle. Pesto is a flavorful sauce made from fresh basil, garlic, Parmesan cheese, olive oil, and pine nuts. The combination of zucchini noodles and pesto creates a light and flavorful meal that is packed with nutrition. The pesto adds a zesty flavour to the noodles that will zap and zing your mouth. The combination of the two ingredients is a great way to get your daily dose of vegetables and flavour in one meal.

Ingredients:

- 2 medium zucchinis
- 2 tablespoons olive oil
- 2 cloves garlic, minced
- 1/4 cup basil pesto
- Salt and pepper, to taste
- 1/4 cup freshly grated Parmesan cheese

Instructions:

1. Using a spiralizer, julienne peeler, or mandoline, cut the zucchini into thin noodles.

2. Heat the olive oil in a large skillet over medium heat. Add the garlic and cook for 1 minute, stirring occasionally.

3. Add the zucchini noodles to the skillet and cook for 3-4 minutes, stirring occasionally, until the noodles are tender.

4. Reduce the heat to low and add the pesto, stirring to combine.

5. Season with salt and pepper, to taste.

6. Serve the zucchini noodles with a sprinkle of Parmesan cheese. Enjoy!

Cauliflower Rice

Cauliflower Rice is a healthy alternative to traditional white rice because it is low in calories and carbohydrates, and high in fibre, vitamins, and minerals. It is also gluten-free and a great source of antioxidants. Cauliflower Rice is also a great source of dietary fibre, which helps to keep you feeling full for longer and can help with weight loss. Eating Cauliflower Rice can also help to reduce inflammation in the body, improve digestion, and boost your immune system. Furthermore, Cauliflower Rice is a great way to add more vegetables to your diet, which is essential for a healthy lifestyle.

Ingredients:

- 1 head of cauliflower
- 2 tablespoons of olive oil
- Salt and pepper to taste
- 2 cloves garlic, minced
- 1/4 cup of diced onion
- 1/4 cup of diced bell pepper
- 1/4 cup of frozen peas
- 2 tablespoons of soy sauce

Instructions:

1. Preheat the oven to 375 degrees Fahrenheit.

2. Cut cauliflower into small florets and place on a baking sheet. Drizzle with olive oil and season with salt and pepper. Roast for 20 minutes, stirring halfway through.

3. Heat a large skillet over medium heat and add the garlic, onion, and bell pepper. Cook for 3-4 minutes, stirring occasionally.

4. Add the roasted cauliflower to the skillet and stir to combine.

5. Add the frozen peas and soy sauce and stir to combine. Cook for an additional 5 minutes, stirring occasionally.

6. Serve warm and enjoy!

Eggplant Lasagna

Eggplant Lasagna is a fun and healthy alternative to traditional lasagna because it is lower in calories and fat than traditional lasagna, while still providing plenty of flavour. It is also quick and easy to make, and can be enjoyed by all members of the family. Eggplant Lasagna is a great way to get your family to eat more vegetables, as the eggplant provides a delicious and hearty texture. Additionally, this dish can be made ahead of time, making it a great option for busy weeknights.

Ingredients:

- 2 large eggplants, sliced into 1/4-inch thick rounds
- 2 tablespoons olive oil
- 1 onion, chopped
- 2 cloves garlic, minced
- 1 (28-ounce) can crushed tomatoes
- 1 teaspoon dried oregano
- 1 teaspoon dried basil
- 1/2 teaspoon salt
- 1/4 teaspoon black pepper
- 1 (15-ounce) container ricotta cheese
- 1/2 cup grated Parmesan cheese
- 2 cups shredded mozzarella cheese
- 1/4 cup chopped fresh parsley

Instructions:

1. Preheat the oven to 375 degrees F.

2. Arrange eggplant slices on a baking sheet. Brush both sides of each slice with olive oil. Bake for 20 minutes, flipping once halfway through.

3. Meanwhile, heat remaining olive oil in a large skillet over medium-high heat. Add onion and garlic and cook until softened, about 5 minutes.

4. Add crushed tomatoes, oregano, basil, salt, and pepper. Simmer for 10 minutes.

5. In a medium bowl, mix together ricotta cheese, Parmesan cheese, and parsley.

6. Spread 1/3 of the tomato sauce in the bottom of a 9x13-inch baking dish. Arrange half of the eggplant slices over the sauce. Spread half of the ricotta cheese mixture over the eggplant. Top with another 1/3 of the tomato sauce.

7. Arrange the remaining eggplant slices over the sauce. Spread the remaining ricotta cheese mixture over the eggplant. Top with the remaining tomato sauce. Sprinkle it with mozzarella cheese.

8. Bake for 30 minutes, or until the cheese is melted and bubbly. Let stand for 10 minutes before serving. Enjoy!

Keto-Friendly Pizza

Keto-Friendly Pizza is a great alternative to traditional pizza because it is low in carbohydrates and high in healthy fats. It is also quick to make since you don't have to wait for the dough to rise. Plus, it tastes delicious and can be customised with your favourite toppings. So, if you're looking for a fun, healthy alternative to traditional pizza, Keto-Friendly Pizza is definitely worth a try!

Ingredients:

- 1/2 cup almond flour
- 1/4 cup coconut flour
- 1/4 teaspoon baking powder
- 1/4 teaspoon garlic powder
- 1/4 teaspoon Italian seasoning
- 1/4 teaspoon sea salt
- 1/4 cup olive oil
- 1/4 cup water
- 1/2 cup mozzarella cheese, shredded
- 1/4 cup Parmesan cheese, grated
- 1/2 cup sugar-free pizza sauce
- 1/2 cup low-carb vegetables of your choice (mushrooms, bell peppers, onions, etc.)
- 1/4 cup pepperoni slices

Instructions:

1. Preheat the oven to 350 degrees F.

2. In a medium bowl, combine almond flour, coconut flour, baking powder, garlic powder, Italian seasoning, and sea salt.

3. Add olive oil and water to the dry ingredients and mix until a dough forms.

4. Grease a 9-inch round baking pan with olive oil.

5. Spread the dough evenly in the baking pan.

6. Sprinkle mozzarella cheese and Parmesan cheese over the dough.

7. Spread the pizza sauce over the cheese.

8. Top with the vegetables and pepperoni slices.

9. Bake in a preheated oven for 25-30 minutes, or until the crust is golden brown.

10. Let cool for 5 minutes before slicing and serving. Enjoy!

Chapter 2: Quick and Easy Meals

2.1 One-Pot Meals

One-pot meals are a great way to make a delicious dinner with minimal effort because they require minimal preparation and cooking time. All the ingredients are cooked together in one pot, so there is no need to spend time prepping multiple dishes. This makes them an ideal choice for busy weeknights when you don't have a lot of time to spend in the kitchen. Plus, the flavours of the ingredients blend together in the pot, creating a delicious meal that everyone will love. Making a one-pot meal is also incredibly easy. All you need to do is add the ingredients to the pot, bring it to a boil, and then reduce the heat and let it simmer until the ingredients are cooked through.

Over the next few pages are some easy one-pot recipes to try:

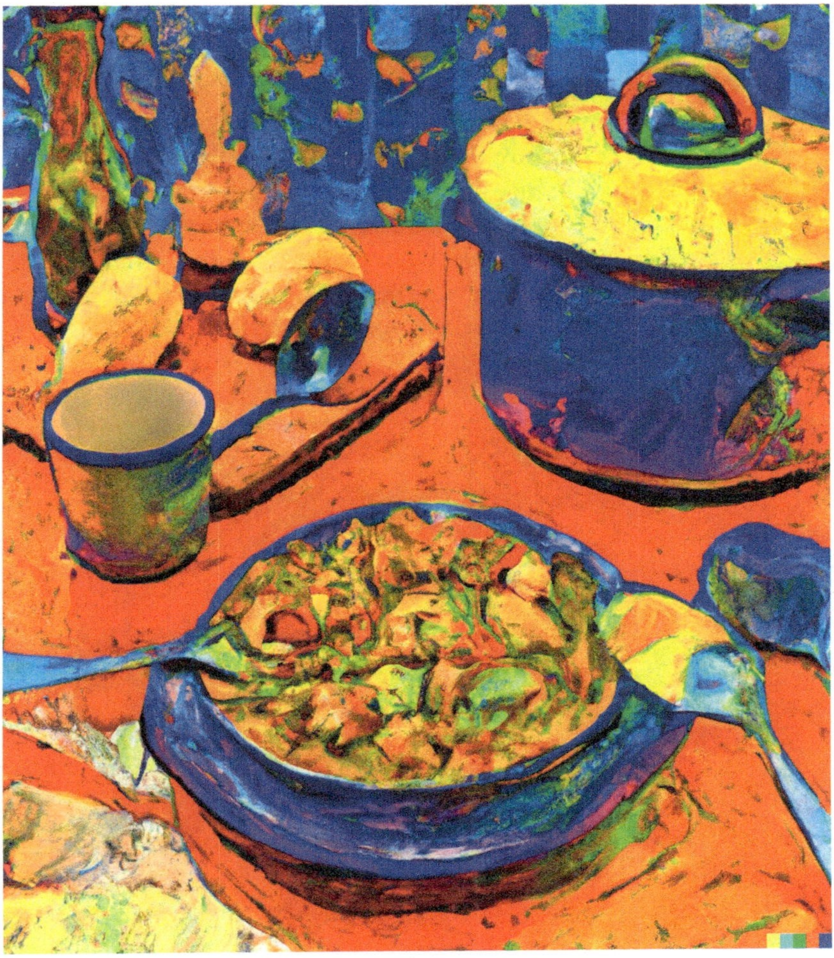

Chicken and Rice

Chicken and Rice is a delicious meal that is both tasty and easy to make. It is a great combination of proteins and carbohydrates, making it a balanced meal. The rice provides a great base for the chicken to be cooked in, and the chicken adds a great flavour. You can easily customise the flavours of the meal by adding spices, herbs, and other ingredients to the mix. It is also a very easy meal to make, as all you need to do is cook the chicken and rice together in a pot. This meal can be made with minimal effort and maximum flavour, making it a great choice for busy nights.

Ingredients:

- 2 tablespoons olive oil
- 1 onion, chopped
- 2 cloves garlic, minced
- 1 red bell pepper, chopped
- 2 cups uncooked long-grain white rice
- 4 cups chicken broth
- 2 teaspoons dried oregano
- 1 teaspoon ground cumin
- 1 teaspoon paprika
- 1/2 teaspoon salt
- 1/4 teaspoon black pepper
- 1/4 teaspoon red pepper flakes
- 2 bay leaves
- 2 boneless, skinless chicken breasts, cut into 1-inch cubes
- 1 (14.5 oz) can diced tomatoes, undrained
- 1 (4 oz) can chopped green chilies
- 1/2 cup frozen corn
- 1/2 cup frozen peas
- 1/4 cup chopped fresh cilantro

Instructions:

1. Heat the oil in a large pot over medium heat. Add the onion and garlic and cook until softened, about 5 minutes.

2. Add the red bell pepper and cook for another 3 minutes.

3. Add the rice, chicken broth, oregano, cumin, paprika, salt, black pepper, red pepper flakes, and bay leaves. Stir to combine.

4. Add the chicken and stir to combine. Bring to a boil, reduce heat to low, cover, and simmer for 15 minutes.

5. Add the diced tomatoes, green chilies, corn, and peas. Stir to combine. Cover and simmer for another 15 minutes, or until the rice is cooked through and the chicken is cooked through.

6. Remove from heat and stir in the cilantro. Serve warm.

Chili One Pot Meal

Chili One Pot Meal is a tasty, quick, fun, and exciting meal that is easy to make. It can be made with a variety of ingredients, so you can customise it to your own tastes. It's also a great meal to make ahead of time and freeze for later. The one-pot meal is also great for busy weeknights since it requires minimal prep and clean up. Plus, it's a hearty and comforting dish that the whole family can enjoy.
Chili One Pot Meal is a great dish for all seasons.

Ingredients:

- 1 tablespoon olive oil
- 1 onion, diced
- 2 cloves garlic, minced
- 1 red bell pepper, diced
- 1 jalapeno pepper, diced
- 1 pound ground beef
- 2 tablespoons chilli powder
- 1 teaspoon cumin
- 1 teaspoon oregano
- 1 teaspoon smoked paprika
- 1/2 teaspoon salt
- 1/4 teaspoon black pepper
- 1 (14.5 ounce) can diced tomatoes
- 1 (15 ounce) can black beans, drained and rinsed
- 1 (15 ounce) can corn, drained
- 1 cup beef broth
- 1/4 cup chopped fresh cilantro

Instructions:

1. Heat the olive oil in a large pot over medium heat. Add the onion, garlic, bell pepper, and jalapeno pepper. Cook until the vegetables are softened, about 5 minutes.

2. Add the ground beef and cook until browned, about 8 minutes.

3. Add the chilli powder, cumin, oregano, smoked paprika, salt, and black pepper. Stir to combine.

4. Add the diced tomatoes, black beans, corn, and beef broth. Bring to a boil, then reduce the heat and simmer for 15 minutes.

5. Garnish with cilantro and serve.

Cheesy Mac and Bacon One-Pot Meal

Cheesy Mac and Bacon One-Pot Meal is a delicious and easy-to-make meal that is sure to please both kids and adults alike. The combination of macaroni, cheese, and bacon creates a savoury and comforting dish that is sure to satisfy everyone's cravings. The one-pot method of cooking also makes it a quick and easy meal to prepare, making it a great option for busy weeknights. Plus, the bacon adds a nice smoky flavour and crunchy texture that makes it even more enjoyable.

Ingredients:

- 2 tablespoons olive oil
- 1 small onion, diced
- 4 cloves garlic, minced
- 2 cups uncooked macaroni
- 4 cups chicken broth • 1/2 teaspoon dried thyme
- 1/2 teaspoon dried oregano
- 1/2 teaspoon ground black pepper
- 2 cups shredded sharp cheddar cheese
- 4 slices cooked bacon, crumbled
- 1/4 cup grated Parmesan cheese

Instructions:

1. Heat the olive oil in a large pot over medium heat.

2. Add the onion and garlic and cook until softened, about 5 minutes.

3. Add the macaroni, chicken broth, thyme, oregano, and black pepper.

4. Bring to a boil, then reduce heat to low and simmer, stirring occasionally, until the macaroni is cooked through, about 10 minutes.

5. Remove from heat and stir in the cheddar cheese and bacon.

6. Sprinkle the Parmesan cheese on top.

7. Serve hot. Enjoy!

Beef Stew

Beef Stew is tasty and good honest food because it is a hearty, comforting meal that is packed with flavour and nutrition. It is made with slow-cooked beef, vegetables, and a flavorful broth that is simmered for hours. The beef and vegetables are cooked until they are tender and the flavours meld together to create a delicious and filling meal. Beef Stew is also a great way to stretch your grocery budget, as it is a great way to use up leftover beef and vegetables. Plus, it is a great meal to make ahead and freeze for later.

Ingredients:

- 1 tablespoon olive oil
- 2 pounds beef stew meat, cubed
- 1 large onion, diced
- 3 cloves garlic, minced
- 3 carrots, peeled and diced
- 3 stalks celery, diced
- 2 potatoes, peeled and diced
- 1 teaspoon dried thyme
- 1 teaspoon dried rosemary
- 1 teaspoon dried oregano
- 1 teaspoon paprika
- 1 teaspoon salt
- 1/2 teaspoon black pepper
- 2 cups beef broth
- 1 (14.5 ounce) can diced tomatoes
- 2 tablespoons tomato paste
- 2 tablespoons Worcestershire sauce
- 2 tablespoons all-purpose flour
- 1/4 cup cold water

Instructions:

1. Heat the olive oil in a large pot over medium-high heat. Add the beef and cook until browned, about 5 minutes.

2. Add the onion, garlic, carrots, celery, potatoes, thyme, rosemary, oregano, paprika, salt, and pepper. Cook for about 5 minutes, stirring occasionally.

3. Add the beef broth, diced tomatoes, tomato paste, and Worcestershire sauce. Bring to a boil, then reduce the heat to low and simmer for 1 hour, stirring occasionally.

4. In a small bowl, whisk together the flour and cold water until smooth. Slowly add the flour mixture to the stew, stirring constantly until thickened.

5. Simmer for an additional 15 minutes, stirring occasionally. Serve warm.

2.2 Sheet Pan Dinners

Sheet pan dinners are a great way to make a delicious meal with minimal effort. They are incredibly easy to make, as all the ingredients are placed on one sheet pan, which is then placed in the oven. This makes for an easy clean-up, as there is only one pan to wash. Additionally, the ingredients can be arranged in such a way that they cook evenly and absorb maximum flavour. You can also add spices and herbs to the ingredients to give the meal even more flavour. Sheet pan dinners are a great way to make a delicious, flavorful meal with minimal effort.

Over the next few pages are some delicious sheet pan dinners to try:

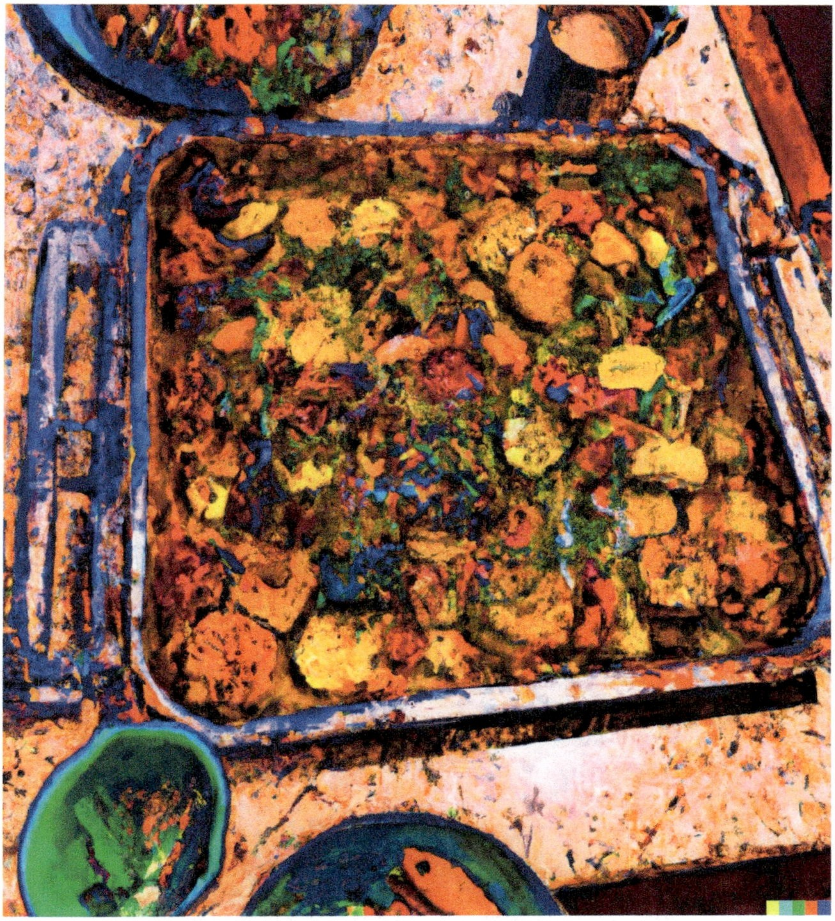

Roasted Vegetables

Roasted vegetables are a great way to get your daily dose of vitamins and minerals. They are also a great source of fibre, which can help with digestion and weight management. Roasting vegetables brings out their natural sweetness and enhances their flavour, making them a delicious accompaniment to any dish. Roasting also helps to retain more of the nutrients in the vegetables, so you get more of the health benefits. Plus, they are easy to make and can be a fun and creative way to add some variety to your meals.

Ingredients:

- 2 tablespoons olive oil
- 1 teaspoon garlic powder
- 1 teaspoon onion powder
- 1 teaspoon dried oregano
- 1 teaspoon dried thyme
- 1/2 teaspoon smoked paprika
- 1/2 teaspoon ground cumin
- 1/2 teaspoon salt
- 1/4 teaspoon black pepper
- 2 large sweet potatoes, peeled and cut into 1-inch cubes
- 2 large carrots, peeled and cut into 1-inch cubes
- 1 large red onion, cut into 1-inch cubes
- 1 red bell pepper, cut into 1-inch cubes
- 1 yellow bell pepper, cut into 1-inch cubes
- 1 zucchini, cut into 1-inch cubes
- 1/2 cup cherry tomatoes

Instructions:

1. Preheat the oven to 425°F. Line a large baking sheet with parchment paper.

2. In a small bowl, mix together olive oil, garlic powder, onion powder, oregano, thyme, smoked paprika, cumin, salt, and pepper.

3. Place sweet potatoes, carrots, red onion, bell peppers, zucchini, and cherry tomatoes on the prepared baking sheet. Drizzle with olive oil mixture and toss to combine.

4. Roast in a preheated oven for 25 minutes, stirring halfway through. Serve warm. Enjoy!

Baked Salmon

Baked Salmon is a great source of protein, healthy fats, and essential vitamins and minerals. It is high in omega-3 fatty acids, which are important for heart health, brain function, and joint health. Salmon also contains high levels of vitamin D, which helps to strengthen bones and teeth. Additionally, salmon is low in calories and saturated fat, making it a healthy choice for those looking to lose weight or maintain a healthy lifestyle.

Ingredients:

-4 (6-ounce) salmon fillets

- 2 tablespoons olive oil
- 1 teaspoon lemon zest
- 2 tablespoons freshly squeezed lemon juice
- 2 cloves garlic, minced
- 1 teaspoon dried oregano
- 1 teaspoon dried thyme
- 1/2 teaspoon sea salt
- 1/4 teaspoon freshly ground black pepper
- 2 cups baby potatoes, halved
- 1 red bell pepper, cut into 1-inch pieces
- 1 yellow bell pepper, cut into 1-inch pieces
- 1/2 cup pitted kalamata olives
- 2 tablespoons chopped fresh parsley

Instructions:

1. Preheat the oven to 400°F.

2. Place salmon fillets in a single layer on a large baking sheet.

3. In a small bowl, whisk together olive oil, lemon zest, lemon juice, garlic, oregano, thyme, salt, and pepper.

4. Drizzle the olive oil mixture over the salmon fillets.

5. Arrange the potatoes, bell peppers, and olives around the salmon.

6. Bake in a preheated oven for 20 minutes, or until the salmon is cooked through and the potatoes are tender.

7. Sprinkle with fresh parsley before serving. Enjoy!

Chicken Fajitas

Chicken Fajitas are a fun and relaxing food because they are easy to make and customise, they are full of flavour, and they can be enjoyed in a variety of ways. They are also a great way to get creative with your meal and make it your own. Plus, they are a great way to get the whole family involved in the cooking process.

Ingredients:

- 1 lb boneless, skinless chicken breasts, cut into strips
- 1 red bell pepper, cut into strips
- 1 green bell pepper, cut into strips
- 1 onion, cut into strips
- 2 tablespoons olive oil
- 1 teaspoon garlic powder
- 1 teaspoon chilli powder
- 1 teaspoon cumin
- 1 teaspoon paprika
- 1 teaspoon oregano
- 1/2 teaspoon salt
- 1/2 teaspoon pepper
- 8-10 flour tortillas

Instructions:

1. Preheat the oven to 400°F.

2. Place chicken, bell peppers, and onion on a large sheet pan. Drizzle with olive oil and season with garlic powder, chilli powder, cumin, paprika, oregano, salt, and pepper. Toss to combine.

3. Bake for 20-25 minutes, stirring halfway through, until chicken is cooked through and vegetables are tender.

4. Serve with warm flour tortillas and your favourite toppings such as salsa, guacamole, sour cream, and cheese. Enjoy!

Sausage and Potatoes

Sausage and potatoes are a fun and comforting food because they are easy to make, full of flavour, and can be enjoyed in a variety of ways. The combination of savoury sausage and starchy potatoes is a classic that can be enjoyed in a variety of dishes, from breakfast skillets to hearty casseroles. Plus, they are both budget-friendly ingredients that can be used to make a delicious meal without breaking the bank.

Ingredients:

- 1 lb. smoked sausage, sliced
- 2 lbs. potatoes, cut into 1-inch cubes
- 1 large onion, chopped
- 2 tablespoons olive oil
- 1 teaspoon garlic powder
- 1 teaspoon dried oregano
- 1 teaspoon dried basil
- 1 teaspoon paprika
- Salt and pepper, to taste

Instructions:

1. Preheat the oven to 400°F.

2. Place the sausage, potatoes, and onion in a large bowl. Drizzle with olive oil and sprinkle with garlic powder, oregano, basil, paprika, salt, and pepper. Toss to combine.

3. Spread the sausage and potatoes onto a large baking sheet.

4. Bake for 25-30 minutes, stirring once halfway through, until the potatoes are tender and the sausage is cooked through.

5. Serve warm. Enjoy!

2.3 Slow Cooker Meals

Slow cooker meals are a fantastic way to make a delicious dinner with minimal effort. Slow cooking allows you to combine all the ingredients into one pot and let them simmer for hours, resulting in a flavorful, tender meal. Slow cooker meals are also incredibly convenient, as they can be prepared ahead of time and left to cook while you are away, so you can come home to a hot, ready-to-eat meal. Plus, slow cooker meals are often budget-friendly, as they use cheaper cuts of meat that become tender and juicy with slow cooking. So if you're looking for a delicious, easy-to-make dinner with minimal effort, look no further than the slow cooker!

Over the next few pages are some easy slow cooker recipes to try:

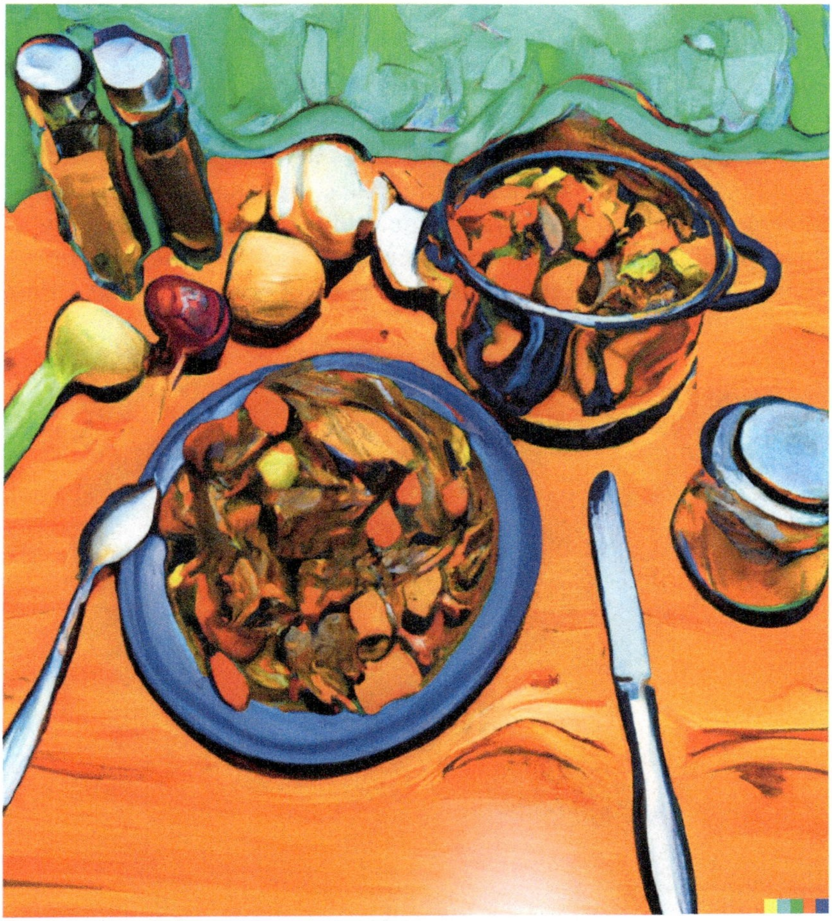

Beef Stroganoff

Beef Stroganoff is a classic comfort food that is sure to please even the pickiest of eaters. It's a hearty and flavorful dish that is easy to make and can be enjoyed any night of the week. The combination of tender beef, mushrooms, and a creamy sauce makes for a delicious and satisfying meal. Plus, the dish is incredibly versatile and can be customised to fit any dietary needs or preferences. Whether you're looking for a quick weeknight dinner or a special occasion meal, Beef Stroganoff is sure to be a hit!

Ingredients:

- 1 1/2 pounds beef stew meat, cut into 1-inch cubes
- 1/4 cup all-purpose flour
- 2 tablespoons olive oil
- 1 large onion, chopped
- 2 cloves garlic, minced
- 1 (8 ounce) package sliced mushrooms
- 1 (10.75 ounce) can condensed cream of mushroom soup
- 1 (10.75 ounce) can condensed French onion soup
- 1/2 cup beef broth
- 1/4 cup dry white wine
- 1 teaspoon Worcestershire sauce
- 1/4 teaspoon ground black pepper
- 1/4 teaspoon dried thyme
- 1/4 teaspoon paprika
- 1/4 teaspoon garlic powder
- 1/4 teaspoon onion powder
- 1/4 cup sour cream
- 2 tablespoons chopped fresh parsley

Instructions:

1. Place the beef cubes in a shallow dish and sprinkle with the flour. Toss to coat. Heat the oil in a large skillet over medium-high heat. Add the beef cubes and cook, stirring occasionally, until browned on all sides. Remove the beef from the skillet and set aside.

3. Add the onion and garlic to the skillet and cook, stirring occasionally, until the onion is softened, about 5 minutes.

4. Add the mushrooms and cook, stirring occasionally, until the mushrooms are softened, about 5 minutes.

5. Return the beef to the skillet and stir in the cream of mushroom soup, French onion soup, beef broth, wine, Worcestershire sauce, pepper, thyme, paprika, garlic powder, and onion powder. Bring the mixture to a boil, then reduce the heat to low and simmer, stirring occasionally, for 1 hour.

6. Transfer the mixture to a slow cooker, cook on low for 4 to 6 hours.

7. Stir in the sour cream and parsley and season with salt and pepper to taste. Serve over egg noodles or mashed potatoes.

Pulled Pork

Pulled pork is a delicious and versatile meal that is perfect for any occasion. It is easy to make and can be served in a variety of ways. The slow-cooked pork is succulent and juicy, and the combination of spices and seasonings make it a flavorful and satisfying meal. Pulled pork is also a great way to feed a crowd, as it can be served as a main dish or as part of a larger meal. With its rich, smoky flavour and tender texture, pulled pork is sure to be a hit at any gathering.

Ingredients:

- 4-5 lb. boneless pork shoulder
- 2 tablespoons olive oil
- 2 tablespoons smoked paprika
- 2 tablespoons garlic powder
- 2 tablespoons onion powder
- 2 tablespoons chilli powder
- 1 teaspoon cumin
- 1 teaspoon black pepper
- 1 teaspoon sea salt
- 1 cup chicken broth
- 1/2 cup apple cider vinegar
- 1/4 cup brown sugar
- 2 tablespoons Worcestershire sauce
- 2 tablespoons Dijon mustard
- 1/4 cup tomato paste

Instructions:

1. In a small bowl, mix together the smoked paprika, garlic powder, onion powder, chilli powder, cumin, black pepper, and sea salt.

2. Rub the pork shoulder with the olive oil and the spice mixture.

3. Place the pork shoulder in a slow cooker.

4. In a medium bowl, whisk together the chicken broth, apple cider vinegar, brown sugar, Worcestershire sauce, Dijon mustard, and tomato paste.

5. Pour the mixture over the pork shoulder.

6. Cook on low for 8-10 hours or high for 4-5 hours, until the pork is tender and shreds easily with a fork.

7. Serve the pulled pork on hamburger buns with your favourite toppings. Enjoy!

Chicken Curry

Chicken Curry is an incredibly flavorful and versatile dish that is sure to please any palate. It is a great meal for any occasion, whether it be a weeknight dinner, a special occasion, or a potluck. The combination of spices, vegetables, and chicken make it a hearty and nutritious meal that is sure to satisfy. Plus, it is easy to make and can be customised to your personal taste. With so many delicious variations to choose from, Chicken Curry is sure to become a favourite in your home.

Ingredients:

- 2 lbs boneless, skinless chicken thighs, cut into 1-inch cubes
- 1 onion, diced
- 2 cloves garlic, minced
- 1 tablespoon fresh ginger, grated
- 2 tablespoons curry powder
- 1 teaspoon ground cumin
- 1 teaspoon ground coriander
- 1 teaspoon ground turmeric
- 1 teaspoon garam masala
- 1/2 teaspoon ground cinnamon
- 1/2 teaspoon cayenne pepper
- 1/2 teaspoon ground cardamom
- 1/4 teaspoon ground cloves
- 1 (14.5 ounce) can diced tomatoes
- 1 (14.5 ounce) can coconut milk
- 1/4 cup chopped fresh cilantro
- Salt and pepper, to taste

Instructions:

1. Place the chicken, onion, garlic, ginger, curry powder, cumin, coriander, turmeric, garam masala, cinnamon, cayenne pepper, cardamom, and cloves in a slow cooker.

2. Pour the diced tomatoes and coconut milk over the chicken.

3. Cover and cook on low for 6-8 hours or on high for 3-4 hours.

4. When the chicken is cooked through, stir in the cilantro and season with salt and pepper to taste.

5. Serve over cooked rice, quinoa, or cauliflower rice. Enjoy!

Chilli

Chilli is a great meal option for a variety of reasons. It is a hearty and flavorful dish that is both nutritious and filling. It is also easy to make and can be customised to suit any dietary needs or preferences. Additionally, it can be made in large batches and frozen for future meals, making it a great option for busy families or individuals. With its combination of protein, vegetables, and spices, chilli is a great way to get a balanced meal that is both delicious and satisfying.

Ingredients:

- 2 pounds ground beef
- 1 large onion, chopped
- 2 cloves garlic, minced
- 1 (15-ounce) can diced tomatoes
- 1 (15-ounce) can tomato sauce
- 1 (4-ounce) can diced green chilies
- 2 tablespoons chilli powder
- 1 teaspoon ground cumin
- 1 teaspoon dried oregano
- 1 teaspoon sugar
- 1/2 teaspoon salt
- 1/4 teaspoon black pepper
- 1/4 teaspoon cayenne pepper
- 1 (15-ounce) can kidney beans, drained and rinsed
- 1 (15-ounce) can black beans, drained and rinsed

Instructions:

1. In a large skillet over medium-high heat, cook the ground beef, onion, and garlic until the beef is no longer pink. Drain off any fat.

2. Transfer the beef mixture to a slow cooker. Add the diced tomatoes, tomato sauce, green chilies, chilli powder, cumin, oregano, sugar, salt, pepper, and cayenne pepper. Stir to combine.

3. Cover and cook on low for 6 to 8 hours.

4. Add the kidney beans and black beans to the slow cooker and stir to combine. Cover and cook for an additional 30 minutes.

5. Serve with your favourite toppings, such as shredded cheese, sour cream, and diced onions. Enjoy!

Chapter 3: Global Cuisines

3.1 Mexican Cuisine

Mexican cuisine is renowned for its vibrant and unique flavours, which are created through the combination of a variety of spices, herbs, and ingredients. Mexican cuisine is full of flavour and spice, making it one of the most popular and beloved cuisines in the world. From the smoky, earthy flavours of chipotle peppers to the bright, citrusy notes of cilantro, Mexican cuisine offers a wide range of flavour profiles that can be enjoyed by everyone. The use of spices such as cumin, chilli powder, and oregano adds a depth of flavour to Mexican dishes that can't be found in any other cuisine. Additionally, Mexican cuisine is known for its use of fresh ingredients, such as tomatoes, onions, and peppers, which add a freshness and zest to the dishes. With its vibrant flavours, Mexican cuisine is sure to tantalise your taste buds and leave you wanting more.

Over the next few pages are some delicious Mexican recipes to try:

Tacos

Tacos are an incredibly versatile and delicious meal that can be enjoyed by everyone. They are easy to make, full of flavour and can be customised to suit any taste. Tacos are a great way to get creative in the kitchen and can be enjoyed as a light snack or a full meal. They are also a great way to get your daily dose of vegetables and protein. With endless possibilities for toppings, fillings, and sauces, tacos are a great way to add variety to your diet. So why not give tacos a try and enjoy a tasty and nutritious meal!

Ingredients:

- 1 lb ground beef
- 1 packet taco seasoning
- 1/2 cup water
- 1/2 cup salsa
- 1/2 cup chopped onion
- 1/2 cup shredded cheese
- 1/2 cup chopped tomatoes
- 1/2 cup sliced black olives
- 1/2 cup shredded lettuce
- 1/2 cup sour cream
- 1/2 cup guacamole
- 8-10 soft taco shells

Instructions:

1. In a large skillet, cook the ground beef over medium heat until it is no longer pink. Drain off any excess fat.

2. Add the taco seasoning and water to the skillet and stir to combine. Simmer for 5 minutes.

3. Add the salsa and onion and cook for an additional 5 minutes.

4. Preheat the oven to 350 degrees F.

5. Place the taco shells on a baking sheet and bake for 5 minutes.

6. Remove the taco shells from the oven and fill each one with the beef mixture.

7. Top the tacos with cheese, tomatoes, olives, lettuce, sour cream, and guacamole.

8. Serve immediately. Enjoy!

Enchiladas

Enchiladas are a delicious and versatile meal that are perfect for sharing with friends and family. They are easy to make, can be filled with a variety of ingredients, and are packed with flavour. Enchiladas are a great way to bring people together, as they can be customised to everyone's individual tastes. Plus, they are a great way to use up leftovers and are a great way to get creative in the kitchen. With enchiladas, you can make a meal that is sure to please everyone.

Ingredients:

- 1 tablespoon olive oil
- 1 onion, diced
- 2 cloves garlic, minced
- 1 pound ground beef
- 1 teaspoon ground cumin
- 1 teaspoon chilli powder
- 1 teaspoon dried oregano
- 1 (10 ounce) can red enchilada sauce
- 1 (4 ounce) can diced green chilies
- 12 (6 inch) corn tortillas
- 1 (8 ounce) package shredded Mexican cheese blend
- 1/2 cup sour cream

Instructions:

1. Preheat the oven to 375 degrees F (190 degrees C).

2. Heat olive oil in a large skillet over medium heat. Add onion and garlic and cook until onion is softened, about 5 minutes. Add ground beef and cook until browned, about 5 minutes more. Drain off any excess fat.

3. Add cumin, chilli powder, and oregano to the beef and stir to combine. Pour in enchilada sauce and diced green chilies and stir to combine. Simmer for 5 minutes.

4. Spread a thin layer of the beef mixture in the bottom of a 9x13 inch baking dish.

5. Place a heaping tablespoon of the beef mixture in the centre of each tortilla. Roll up the tortilla and place it seam side down in the baking dish. Repeat with remaining tortillas.

6. Pour any remaining beef mixture over the enchiladas and sprinkle with the Mexican cheese blend.

7. Bake in a preheated oven for 20 minutes.

8. Serve with sour cream. Enjoy!

Burritos

Burritos are a great meal option for anyone looking for a flavorful and filling meal. Not only are they delicious, but they are also incredibly versatile, allowing you to customise them to your own tastes. Burritos are also a great way to get a variety of nutrients in one meal, as you can fill them with a variety of ingredients such as beans, rice, vegetables, and proteins. They are also incredibly easy to make and can be ready in minutes. All in all, burritos are a great meal choice for anyone looking for a delicious and nutritious meal.

Ingredients:

- 2 tablespoons olive oil
- 1 onion, diced
- 1 red bell pepper, diced
- 1 jalapeno, seeded and diced
- 1 pound ground beef
- 1 teaspoon ground cumin
- 1 teaspoon chilli powder
- 1 teaspoon garlic powder
- 1 teaspoon onion powder
- 1 teaspoon paprika
- 1 teaspoon oregano
- 1 teaspoon salt
- 1/2 teaspoon black pepper
- 1 (15 ounce) can black beans, drained and rinsed
- 1 (14.5 ounce) can diced tomatoes
- 1/2 cup chicken broth
- 1/4 cup chopped fresh cilantro
- 8 (10 inch) flour tortillas
- 2 cups shredded Monterey Jack cheese
- 1/2 cup sour cream

Instructions:

1. Heat the olive oil in a large skillet over medium heat. Add the onion, bell pepper, and jalapeno and cook until softened, about 5 minutes.

2. Add the ground beef and cook until browned, about 5 minutes. Drain off any excess fat.

3. Add the cumin, chilli powder, garlic powder, onion powder, paprika, oregano, salt, and black pepper and stir to combine.

4. Add the black beans, diced tomatoes, and chicken broth and stir to combine. Simmer for 10 minutes.

5. Remove from the heat and stir in the cilantro.

6. Preheat the oven to 350 degrees F (175 degrees C).

7. Place the tortillas on a work surface. Divide the beef mixture among the tortillas, spreading it down the centre. Top with the cheese.

8. Roll up the burritos and place them seam-side down on a baking sheet.

9. Bake for 15 minutes, or until the cheese is melted and the burritos are lightly browned.

10. Serve with sour cream. Enjoy!

Quesadillas

Quesadillas are a great meal option because they are quick, easy, and delicious. They can be customised to fit any dietary preference or taste preference, and can be made with a variety of ingredients. They are also a great way to use up leftovers, as they are a great way to combine different flavours and textures. Quesadillas are a great meal for any time of day, and can be enjoyed as a snack or a full meal.

Ingredients:

- 8-10 flour tortillas
- 2 cups shredded cheese (cheddar, Monterey Jack, or a combination)
- 1/2 cup diced onion
- 1/2 cup diced bell pepper
- 1/2 cup diced tomatoes
- 1/2 cup cooked, crumbled bacon or sausage
- 1/2 cup black beans (optional)
- 1/2 teaspoon cumin
- 1/2 teaspoon chilli powder
- 1/4 teaspoon garlic powder
- 1/4 teaspoon salt
- 1/4 teaspoon pepper
- 2 tablespoons butter

Instructions:

1. Preheat a large skillet over medium heat.

2. Place a tortilla in the skillet and sprinkle with 1/4 cup of the cheese.

3. Top with onion, bell pepper, tomatoes, bacon or sausage, black beans (if desired), cumin, chilli powder, garlic powder, salt, and pepper.

4. Sprinkle with another 1/4 cup of cheese.

5. Place another tortilla on top and press down lightly.

6. Cook for 2-3 minutes, or until lightly browned.

7. Flip and cook for another 2-3 minutes, or until lightly browned.

8. Remove from heat and repeat with remaining ingredients.

9. Serve with salsa, guacamole, sour cream, or your favourite toppings. Enjoy!

3.2 Italian Cuisine

Italian cuisine is renowned for its full-bodied flavour and fresh ingredients. The Mediterranean climate, with its abundance of fresh fruits, vegetables, herbs, and spices, provides the perfect backdrop for delicious Italian dishes. Traditional Italian cooking is based on the use of fresh, seasonal ingredients, prepared with simplicity and care. This results in dishes that are bursting with flavour and texture, making Italian cuisine one of the most popular and beloved cuisines in the world. The combination of fresh ingredients, simple preparation, and bold flavours make Italian cuisine a pleasure to enjoy. From the classic pasta dishes to the more modern creations, Italian cuisine is sure to tantalise your taste buds.

Over the next few pages are some delicious Italian recipes to try:

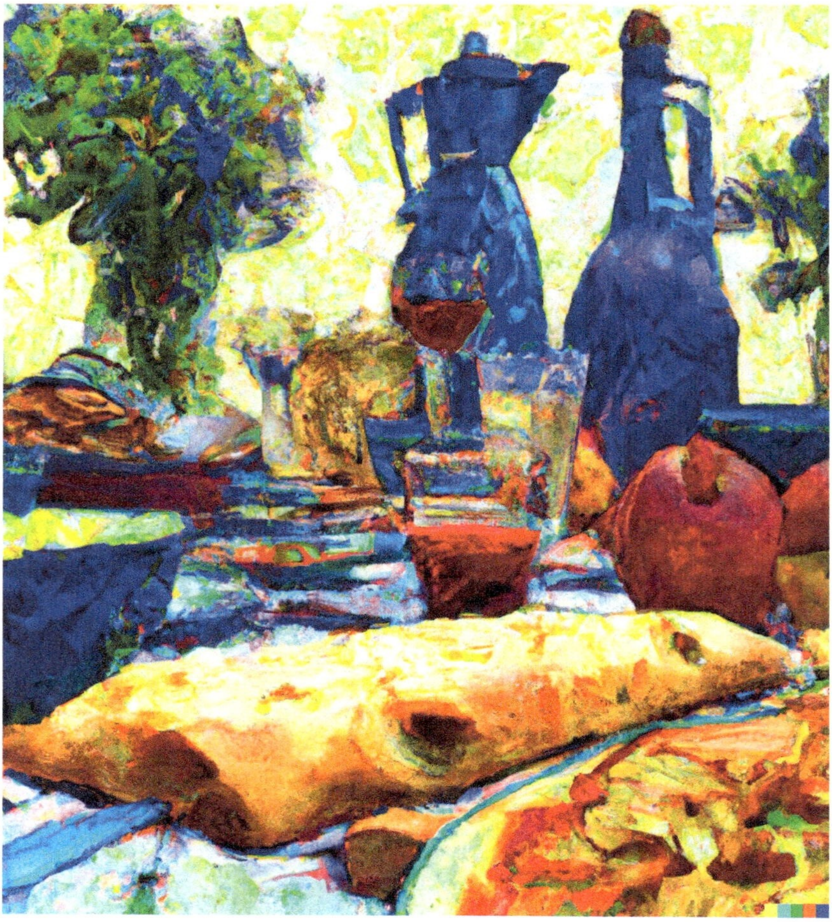

Spaghetti and Meatballs

Spaghetti and Meatballs are a classic dish that is not only delicious but also good for you. This dish is packed with essential nutrients that can help you stay healthy. Spaghetti is a great source of complex carbohydrates, which provide your body with energy and help keep you feeling full longer. Meatballs are a great source of protein, which helps build and repair muscles and other tissues. They are also a good source of iron and zinc, which are important for a healthy immune system. Additionally, the sauce is packed with vitamins and minerals like lycopene and antioxidants, which can help reduce inflammation and protect against disease. All in all, Spaghetti and Meatballs is a great meal that is both delicious and nutritious.

Ingredients:

- 1 lb. ground beef
- 2 cloves garlic, minced
- 1/2 cup bread crumbs
- 1/4 cup grated Parmesan cheese
- 1/4 cup chopped fresh parsley
- 1 egg
- 1 teaspoon dried oregano
- 1 teaspoon dried basil
- 1/2 teaspoon salt
- 1/4 teaspoon black pepper
- 1/4 teaspoon red pepper flakes
- 1/4 cup olive oil
- 1 onion, chopped
- 2 cloves garlic, minced
- 2 (14.5 oz) cans diced tomatoes
- 1 (6 oz) can tomato paste
- 1/2 cup water
- 1/4 teaspoon sugar
- 1/2 teaspoon dried oregano
- 1/2 teaspoon dried basil
- 1/4 teaspoon salt
- 1/4 teaspoon black pepper
- 1/4 teaspoon red pepper flakes
- 1/2 lb. spaghetti
- 1/4 cup grated Parmesan cheese

Instructions:

1. Preheat the oven to 350°F.

2. In a large bowl, combine ground beef, garlic, bread crumbs, Parmesan cheese, parsley, egg, oregano, basil, salt, pepper, and red pepper flakes. Mix until well combined. Shape into 1-inch balls and place on a baking sheet. Bake for 15 minutes.

3. Meanwhile, heat olive oil in a large skillet over medium heat. Add onion and garlic and cook until softened, about 5 minutes.

4. Add tomatoes, tomato paste, water, sugar, oregano, basil, salt, pepper, and red pepper flakes. Bring to a simmer and cook for 10 minutes.

5. Add meatballs to the sauce and simmer for an additional 10 minutes.

6. Bring a large pot of salted water to a boil. Add spaghetti and cook according to package instructions.

7. Serve spaghetti topped with meatballs and sauce. Sprinkle with Parmesan cheese. Enjoy!

Lasagna

Lasagna is an incredibly delicious and nutritious dish that is perfect for any meal. It is made with layers of pasta, cheese, and a variety of meats and vegetables. This combination of ingredients makes lasagna a great source of protein, vitamins, minerals, and fibre. Lasagna is also high in complex carbohydrates, which can help to keep you feeling full for longer. Additionally, the combination of ingredients in lasagna can provide you with a variety of health benefits, such as improved heart health, improved digestion, and increased energy. So if you're looking for a delicious and nutritious meal, look no further than lasagna!

Ingredients:

- 1 pound ground beef
- 1 onion, chopped
- 1 (28 ounce) can crushed tomatoes
- 2 (6 ounce) cans tomato paste
- 2 cloves garlic, minced
- 2 tablespoons white sugar
- 1 teaspoon dried oregano
- 1 teaspoon dried basil
- 1/2 teaspoon ground black pepper and 1/2 teaspoon salt
- 4 tablespoons chopped fresh parsley
- 1 pound lasagna noodles
- 16 ounces ricotta cheese and 1 egg
- 1/2 teaspoon salt
- 3/4 pound mozzarella cheese, sliced
- 3/4 cup grated Parmesan cheese

Instructions:

1. Preheat the oven to 375 degrees F (190 degrees C).

2. In a large skillet, brown the ground beef and onion over medium heat. Drain off excess fat. Stir in crushed tomatoes, tomato paste, garlic, sugar, oregano, basil, pepper, 2 tablespoons parsley, and salt. Simmer, covered, for about 30 minutes, stirring occasionally.

3. Bring a large pot of lightly salted water to a boil. Add lasagna noodles and cook for 8 to 10 minutes or until al dente; drain.

4. In a mixing bowl, combine the ricotta cheese with egg, remaining parsley, and 1/2 teaspoon salt.

5. To assemble, spread 1 1/2 cups of meat sauce in the bottom of a 9x13 inch baking dish. Arrange 6 noodles lengthwise over meat sauce. Spread with one half of the ricotta cheese mixture. Top with a third of mozzarella cheese slices. Spoon 1 1/2 cup meat sauce over mozzarella, and sprinkle with 1/4 cup Parmesan cheese. Repeat layers, and top with remaining mozzarella and Parmesan cheese.

6. Cover with foil: to prevent sticking, either spray foil with cooking spray, or make sure the foil does not touch the cheese.

7. Bake in a preheated oven for 25 minutes. Remove foil, and bake for an additional 25 minutes. Cool for 15 minutes before serving.

Pizza base

Making your own pizza base is a great way to enjoy a delicious and nutritious meal. Not only is it a fun activity to do with family and friends, but it also allows you to customise your pizza to your own tastes. You can choose the type of flour, the amount of yeast, and the amount of oil or butter to make the perfect crust. You can also add herbs, spices, and other ingredients to make a unique and flavorful pizza. Making your own pizza base is also a great way to save money since you can make a large batch of dough and freeze it for future use. Plus, you can be sure that the ingredients you are using are fresh and of the highest quality.

Ingredients:

- 1 1/2 cups all-purpose flour
- 1 teaspoon sugar
- 1 teaspoon salt
- 1 teaspoon active dry yeast
- 3/4 cup warm water
- 2 tablespoons olive oil

Instructions:

1. In a large bowl, mix together the flour, sugar, salt, and yeast.

2. Add the warm water and olive oil and mix until a dough forms.

3. Knead the dough on a lightly floured surface for 5 minutes.

4. Place the dough in a greased bowl, cover with a damp cloth, and let rise for 1 hour.

5. Preheat the oven to 425°F (220°C).

6. Roll out the dough on a lightly floured surface to the desired size and thickness.

7. Place the dough on a greased pizza pan or baking sheet.

8. Top with desired toppings and bake for 15-20 minutes, or until the crust is golden brown.

Pizza

Making your own pizza is a great way to get creative in the kitchen and enjoy a delicious meal. Not only is it a fun activity, but it also allows you to customise your pizza to your exact tastes. You can choose your favourite toppings, experiment with different dough recipes, and even create unique flavour combinations. Plus, making your own pizza is a great way to save money and time. You can make a delicious pizza in the comfort of your own home without having to wait in line or pay for delivery. So, if you're looking for a fun and delicious activity to try, why not give homemade pizza a try?

Ingredients:

- 1 pound store-bought pizza dough or use your pizza base you have made
- 1/2 cup pizza sauce
- 1 cup shredded mozzarella cheese
- 1/4 cup grated Parmesan cheese
- 1/2 cup sliced mushrooms
- 1/2 cup sliced bell peppers
- 1/4 cup sliced black olives
- 1/4 cup chopped onion

Instructions:

1. Preheat the oven to 425°F.

2. On a lightly floured surface, roll out pizza dough to a 12-inch circle. Place on a greased baking sheet.

3. Spread pizza sauce over dough. Sprinkle it with mozzarella and Parmesan cheeses.

4. Top with mushrooms, bell peppers, olives, and onion.

5. Bake for 15 to 20 minutes, or until the crust is golden brown and cheese is melted and bubbly.

6. Slice and serve. Enjoy!

Stuffed Shells

Stuffed Shells are a delicious and nutritious meal that is great fun to make. Not only are they tasty, but they are also packed with nutrition. They are made with a variety of ingredients, including cheese, vegetables, and lean meats, which makes them a great source of protein, vitamins, and minerals. Plus, they are a great way to get creative in the kitchen and make something unique and delicious. Whether you are feeding a family or just yourself, stuffed shells are a great way to get a healthy and delicious meal.

Ingredients:

- 1 box jumbo pasta shells
- 1 lb ground beef
- 1/2 cup chopped onion
- 1/2 cup chopped green pepper
- 1/2 tsp garlic powder
- 1/2 tsp Italian seasoning
- 1/2 tsp salt
- 1/4 tsp pepper
- 1 (15 oz) container ricotta cheese
- 1/2 cup grated Parmesan cheese
- 1 egg
- 2 cups shredded mozzarella cheese
- 1 (26 oz) jar spaghetti sauce

Instructions:

1. Preheat the oven to 350°F.

2. Cook pasta shells according to package directions. Drain and set aside.

3. In a large skillet, cook beef, onion, green pepper, garlic powder, Italian seasoning, salt, and pepper over medium heat until beef is no longer pink. Drain fat.

4. In a medium bowl, mix together ricotta cheese, Parmesan cheese, and egg.

5. Spoon a heaping tablespoon of the cheese mixture into each cooked shell.

6. Place stuffed shells in a 9x13 inch baking dish.

7. Pour spaghetti sauce over shells.

8. Sprinkle it with mozzarella cheese.

9. Bake in a preheated oven for 25 minutes, or until the cheese is melted and bubbly.

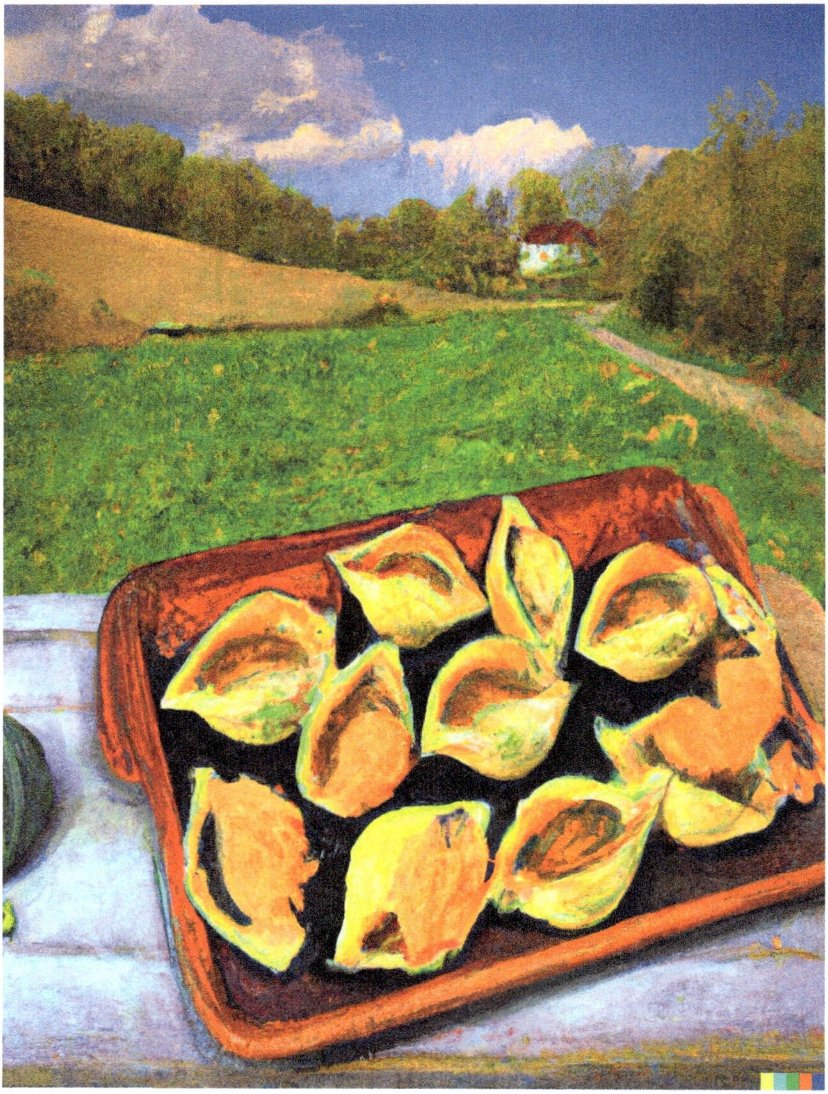

3.3 Asian Cuisine

Asian cuisine is renowned for its fresh ingredients and bold flavours. From the spicy curries of India to the sweet and sour dishes of China, the variety of flavours and ingredients used in Asian cuisine is truly remarkable. The combination of fresh vegetables, herbs and spices, along with the use of traditional cooking techniques, creates dishes that are both flavourful and healthy. Asian cuisine also uses a variety of cooking methods, such as stir-frying, steaming and deep-frying, to bring out the best in the ingredients. This ensures that the dishes are full of flavour and nutrition. Furthermore, Asian cuisine often incorporates a variety of condiments, such as soy sauce, fish sauce and chilli paste, to add an extra layer of flavour to the dishes. With its vibrant flavours and fresh ingredients, Asian cuisine is sure to tantalise your taste buds.

Over the next few pages are some delicious Asian recipes to try:

Stir-Fry

Stir-fry is an incredibly versatile and nutritious meal that can be tailored to fit any dietary needs. It's quick and easy to make, and it's a great way to use up any leftover vegetables you may have in your fridge. Stir-fry is also packed with vitamins, minerals, and fibre, making it a great choice for a healthy meal. Plus, you can customise your stir-fry with different meats, vegetables, and sauces to make it as flavorful as you'd like. If you're looking for a delicious and nutritious meal that's easy to make, stir-fry is the perfect choice.

Ingredients:

- 1 tablespoon vegetable oil
- 1/2 onion, diced
- 1 red bell pepper, diced
- 1 cup broccoli florets
- 1 cup sliced mushrooms
- 2 cloves garlic, minced
- 1/2 teaspoon ground ginger
- 1/4 teaspoon crushed red pepper flakes
- 1/4 cup soy sauce
- 1/4 cup water
- 1/4 cup hoisin sauce
- 1 tablespoon cornstarch
- 2 cups cooked white rice
- 1/4 cup chopped green onions

Instructions:

1. Heat oil in a large skillet over medium-high heat.

2. Add onion, bell pepper, broccoli, and mushrooms. Cook, stirring occasionally, until vegetables are tender, about 5 minutes.

3. Add garlic, ginger, and red pepper flakes. Cook, stirring, for 1 minute.

4. In a small bowl, whisk together soy sauce, water, hoisin sauce, and cornstarch.

5. Pour soy sauce mixture into the skillet and stir to combine.

6. Reduce heat to low and simmer for 5 minutes, stirring occasionally.

7. Serve stir-fry over cooked white rice and sprinkle with green onions. Enjoy!

Fried Rice

Fried Rice is a great meal choice for those looking for a tasty and economical meal. It is a versatile dish that can be made with a variety of ingredients, allowing for a wide range of flavours and textures. Fried Rice is also a great way to use up leftovers, making it an economical choice. Additionally, it is a quick and easy meal to make, making it a great choice for busy weeknights. With its delicious flavour and affordability, Fried Rice is a great meal choice for any occasion.

Ingredients:

- 2 cups cooked white rice
- 2 tablespoons sesame oil
- 1/2 cup diced onion
- 1/2 cup diced carrots
- 1/2 cup frozen peas
- 2 cloves garlic, minced
- 2 tablespoons soy sauce
- 2 tablespoons oyster sauce
- 2 eggs, lightly beaten
- 2 green onions, chopped

Instructions:

1. Heat sesame oil in a large skillet over medium-high heat.

2. Add onions, carrots, and peas and cook until vegetables are tender, about 5 minutes.

3. Add garlic and cook for an additional minute.

4. Add cooked rice and stir to combine.

5. Add soy sauce and oyster sauce and stir to combine.

6. Push the rice mixture to one side of the skillet and add beaten eggs. Cook until eggs are scrambled, about 3 minutes.

7. Stir the eggs into the rice mixture and cook for an additional 2 minutes.

8. Add green onions and stir to combine.

9. Serve hot. Enjoy!

Noodle Soup

Noodle Soup is a great meal choice for those looking for a tasty yet affordable meal. It's easy to make and can be customised to suit any taste. With a variety of different noodles and broths, you can make a delicious soup that is both nutritious and budget-friendly. Plus, it's a great way to use up leftovers and make a meal out of them. Noodle Soup is a great choice for anyone looking for a delicious and inexpensive meal.

Ingredients:

- 8 cups chicken broth
- 1 tablespoon sesame oil
- 2 cloves garlic, minced
- 1 tablespoon fresh ginger, grated
- 2 tablespoons soy sauce
- 2 tablespoons rice vinegar
- 2 tablespoons fish sauce
- 1 teaspoon sugar
- 2 tablespoons vegetable oil
- 1 onion, diced
- 2 carrots, diced
- 2 celery stalks, diced
- 8 ounces mushrooms, sliced
- 8 ounces egg noodles
- 2 cups cooked chicken, shredded
- 2 tablespoons fresh cilantro, chopped

Instructions:

1. In a large pot, heat the chicken broth over medium heat.

2. Add the sesame oil, garlic, ginger, soy sauce, rice vinegar, fish sauce, and sugar. Stir to combine.

3. In a separate pan, heat the vegetable oil over medium heat. Add the onion, carrots, celery, and mushrooms. Cook until the vegetables are softened, about 5 minutes.

4. Add the vegetables to the pot with the broth. Bring to a boil.

5. Add the egg noodles and cook until al dente, about 8 minutes.

6. Add the chicken and cilantro and cook for an additional 2 minutes.

7. Serve hot. Enjoy!

Dumplings

Dumplings are a delicious and versatile meal that can be enjoyed by everyone. They are easy to make and can be filled with a variety of ingredients, making them a great option for a quick and tasty meal. Dumplings are also a great way to use up leftovers, as they can be filled with anything from vegetables to meats. Plus, they can be cooked in a variety of ways, from steaming to frying, making them a great option for any meal. Whether you're looking for a quick snack or a full meal, dumplings are a great choice.

Ingredients:

- 1 package of wonton wrappers
- 1 lb ground pork
- 1/2 cup finely chopped cabbage
- 1/4 cup finely chopped carrots
- 1/4 cup finely chopped green onions
- 2 cloves garlic, minced
- 1 teaspoon fresh ginger, minced
- 2 tablespoons soy sauce
- 1 teaspoon sesame oil
- 1/4 teaspoon white pepper

Instructions:

1. In a large bowl, combine the ground pork, cabbage, carrots, green onions, garlic, ginger, soy sauce, sesame oil, and white pepper. Mix until everything is well combined.

2. To assemble the dumplings, place a wonton wrapper on a flat surface. Place a heaping teaspoon of the pork mixture in the centre of the wrapper.

3. Wet the edges of the wrapper with a little water. Fold the wrapper in half and press the edges together to seal.

4. Heat a large skillet over medium-high heat. Add a tablespoon of oil and swirl to coat the bottom of the pan.

5. Add the dumplings to the skillet and cook until golden brown, about 2 minutes per side.

6. Serve the dumplings with your favourite dipping sauce. Enjoy!

Chapter 4:

Desserts

4.1 No-Bake Desserts

No-bake desserts are a great way to make a delicious treat with minimal effort. They are perfect for busy days when you don't have time to bake, or for when you want to make something special without having to turn on the oven. No-bake desserts are also great for those who don't have access to an oven, as they can be made with just a few ingredients and a few minutes of prep time. Plus, they are often healthier than traditional baked desserts, as they are often made with natural ingredients like fruits, nuts, and oats. So if you're looking for a quick and easy way to make a delicious treat, no-bake desserts are the way to go!

Over the next few pages are some easy no-bake recipes to try:

Chocolate Peanut Butter Bars

Chocolate Peanut Butter Bars are an unbeatable combination of two classic flavours. They are a delicious and indulgent treat that is sure to satisfy any sweet tooth. The combination of creamy peanut butter and rich chocolate creates a decadent flavour that is sure to please. The bars are easy to make and require minimal ingredients, making them a great dessert option for any occasion. Plus, they are sure to be a hit with both kids and adults alike!

Ingredients:

- 2 cups graham cracker crumbs
- 1/2 cup melted butter
- 1/2 cup peanut butter
- 1/2 cup sugar
- 2 cups semi-sweet chocolate chips
- 1/2 cup heavy cream
- 1 teaspoon vanilla extract

Instructions:

1. Preheat the oven to 350°F (175°C).

2. In a medium bowl, combine graham cracker crumbs, melted butter, peanut butter, and sugar. Mix until well blended.

3. Press mixture into a 9x13 inch baking dish. Bake for 10 minutes.

4. In a medium saucepan, combine chocolate chips and cream. Heat over low heat, stirring until melted and smooth.

5. Remove from heat and stir in vanilla extract.

6. Pour melted chocolate over graham cracker crust. Spread evenly.

7. Refrigerate for at least 2 hours before cutting into bars. Enjoy!

Cheesecake

Cheesecake is an amazing dessert that is sure to please everyone. It is a classic dessert that has been around for centuries, and it is still as popular as ever. It is creamy, rich, and delicious, and can be made in a variety of flavours and styles. Cheesecake is a great dessert for any occasion, from a casual gathering to a formal dinner. It is also a great way to end a meal with something sweet. Cheesecake is a great dessert because it is easy to make, it can be made ahead of time, and it is sure to please any crowd.

Ingredients:

Crust:

- 1 ½ cups graham cracker crumbs
- ½ cup melted butter
- 3 tablespoons sugar

Filling:

- 3 (8 ounce) packages cream cheese, softened
- 1 cup sugar
- 3 tablespoons all-purpose flour
- 3 eggs
- 1 teaspoon vanilla extract
- 1 cup sour cream

Instructions:

1. Preheat the oven to 350 degrees F (175 degrees C).

2. In a medium bowl, mix together graham cracker crumbs, melted butter and sugar. Press into the bottom of a 9 inch springform pan.

3. In a large bowl, beat cream cheese until smooth. Gradually beat in sugar and flour. Beat in eggs one at a time, then stir in vanilla and sour cream. Pour filling into the prepared crust.

4. Bake in a preheated oven for 45 minutes. Turn the oven off, and let cheesecake cool in the oven with the door closed for 5 to 6 hours; this prevents cracking. Chill in the refrigerator until serving.

Fudge

Fudge is a delicious and indulgent treat that is perfect for any occasion. It's creamy, rich, and oh-so-sweet, making it a great way to end a meal or provide a special treat for a special occasion. Fudge is also incredibly versatile, with endless flavour combinations and textures that can be tailored to any taste. Whether you prefer a classic chocolate fudge, a nutty peanut butter fudge, or a fruity raspberry swirl, there's a fudge for everyone. Fudge also makes a great gift, as it can be made in advance and stored for weeks. So if you're looking for a delicious and indulgent dessert that everyone will love, fudge is the perfect choice.

Ingredients:

- 3 cups of granulated sugar
- 1/2 cup of butter
- 1/2 cup of evaporated milk
- 2 tablespoons of light corn syrup
- 1/4 teaspoon of salt
- 2 cups of semi-sweet chocolate chips
- 1 teaspoon of vanilla extract
- 1/2 cup of chopped nuts (optional)

Instructions:

1. Grease an 8-inch square baking pan and set aside.

2. In a medium saucepan, combine the sugar, butter, evaporated milk, corn syrup, and salt. Bring to a boil over medium heat, stirring constantly. Boil for 5 minutes, stirring constantly.

3. Remove from heat and add the chocolate chips, stirring until melted. Stir in the vanilla and nuts.

4. Pour the mixture into the prepared pan and spread evenly. Let cool for at least 2 hours before cutting into squares. Enjoy!

Rice Krispie Treats

Rice Krispie Treats are a classic dessert that have been around for decades. They are easy to make, delicious, and incredibly versatile. Rice Krispie Treats are the perfect treat for any occasion, from birthday parties to family gatherings. They can be customised with different flavours, colours, and decorations to suit any taste. Plus, they are a great way to use up leftover cereal. Rice Krispie Treats are a delicious and convenient dessert that everyone can enjoy.

Ingredients:

- 6 cups Rice Krispies cereal
- 10 ounces marshmallows
- 3 tablespoons butter
- 1 teaspoon vanilla extract

Instructions:

1. Grease a 9x13 inch baking dish with butter or cooking spray.

2. In a large pot, melt the butter over low heat.

3. Add the marshmallows and stir until completely melted.

4. Remove from heat and stir in the vanilla extract.

5. Add the Rice Krispies cereal and stir until evenly coated.

6. Transfer the mixture to the prepared baking dish and press down evenly.

7. Allow to cool before cutting into bars. Enjoy!

4.2 Gluten-Free Desserts

As more and more people are becoming aware of the potential health risks associated with consuming gluten, the demand for gluten-free desserts has been steadily increasing. People are now more conscious of their dietary needs and are looking for ways to enjoy their favourite desserts without compromising their health. Gluten-free desserts are becoming increasingly popular because they provide a delicious and safe alternative to traditional desserts that contain gluten. They are also suitable for those with celiac disease, gluten sensitivities, and other dietary restrictions. With the wide variety of gluten-free desserts now available, it is easier than ever to enjoy a delicious treat without the worry of adverse health effects.

Over the next few pages are some delicious gluten-free recipes to try:

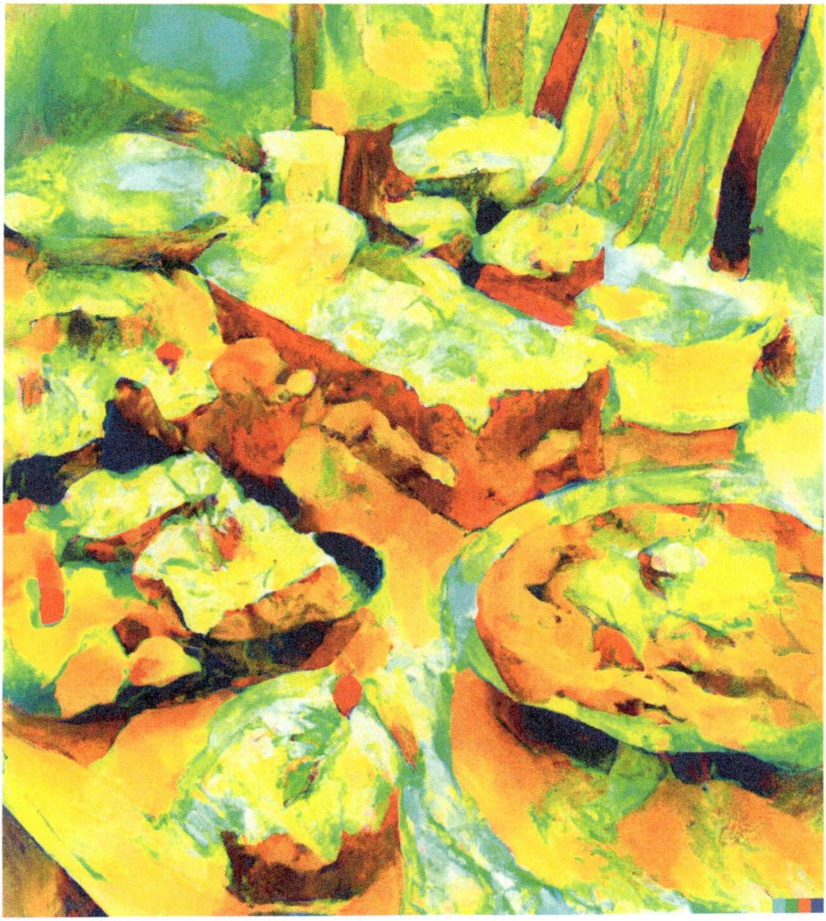

Almond Flour Cookies

Almond flour cookies are a delicious and healthy dessert option. They are made with almond flour, which is a gluten-free alternative to traditional wheat flour. The almond flour gives the cookies a nutty flavour and a chewy texture, making them a great choice for those who are looking for a healthier alternative to regular cookies. Almond flour is also high in protein and fibre, making these cookies a great snack or dessert. Plus, they are easy to make and can be customised with your favourite mix-ins. With almond flour cookies, you can enjoy a guilt-free treat that is sure to satisfy your sweet tooth.

Ingredients:

- 2 cups almond flour
- 1/2 teaspoon baking soda
- 1/4 teaspoon salt
- 1/2 cup butter, softened
- 1/2 cup coconut sugar
- 1 teaspoon vanilla extract
- 1 large egg
- 1/2 cup dark chocolate chips

Instructions:

1. Preheat the oven to 350 degrees F. Line a baking sheet with parchment paper.

2. In a medium bowl, whisk together almond flour, baking soda, and salt.

3. In a large bowl, cream together butter and coconut sugar until light and fluffy. Beat in vanilla extract and egg until combined.

4. Gradually add in almond flour mixture, mixing until just combined. Stir in chocolate chips.

5. Drop dough by tablespoonfuls onto the prepared baking sheet. Bake for 8-10 minutes, or until the edges are golden brown.

6. Let cool on a baking sheet for 5 minutes before transferring to a wire rack to cool completely. Enjoy!

Apple Crisp

Apple Crisp is an amazing dessert that is perfect for any occasion. It is incredibly easy to make, and requires minimal ingredients. The combination of sweet apples and crunchy cinnamon-flavoured topping is a classic flavour that is sure to please any crowd. Apple Crisp is also a great way to use up any extra apples you may have lying around. Plus, it's a great way to get your kids involved in the kitchen! With its delicious flavour and ease of preparation, Apple Crisp is an excellent dessert option.

Ingredients:

- 4 cups peeled and sliced apples
- 1/2 cup light brown sugar
- 1/2 cup all-purpose flour
- 1/2 teaspoon ground cinnamon
- 1/4 teaspoon ground nutmeg
- 1/4 teaspoon salt
- 1/2 cup cold butter, cut into small cubes
- 1/2 cup old-fashioned oats
- 1/2 cup chopped walnuts or pecans (optional)

Instructions:

1. Preheat the oven to 375°F. Grease an 8-inch square baking dish.

2. In a large bowl, combine apples, brown sugar, flour, cinnamon, nutmeg, and salt. Mix until apples are evenly coated.

3. Add butter cubes and mix with a fork or pastry cutter until mixture resembles coarse crumbs.

4. Stir in oats and nuts, if using.

5. Pour mixture into prepared baking dish and spread evenly.

6. Bake for 30-35 minutes, or until the topping is golden brown and apples are tender.

7. Serve warm with ice cream or whipped cream, if desired. Enjoy!

Chocolate Cake

Chocolate Cake is an excellent choice for a dessert. It is a classic and timeless treat that is sure to please everyone. The rich, indulgent flavour of chocolate is sure to satisfy even the most discerning sweet tooth. Chocolate Cake is also incredibly versatile, allowing you to customise it with different frostings, fillings, and toppings to create a unique and delicious treat. Whether you're looking for a simple dessert to share with friends or an elaborate showstopper for a special occasion, Chocolate Cake is sure to be a hit.

Ingredients:

- 2 cups all-purpose flour
- 2 cups white sugar
- 3/4 cup cocoa powder
- 2 teaspoons baking soda
- 1 teaspoon baking powder
- 1 teaspoon salt
- 2 eggs
- 1 cup buttermilk
- 1 cup vegetable oil
- 2 teaspoons vanilla extract
- 1 cup boiling water

Instructions:

1. Preheat the oven to 350 degrees F (175 degrees C). Grease and flour a 9x13 inch pan.

2. In a large bowl, mix together the flour, sugar, cocoa, baking soda, baking powder, and salt.

3. In a separate bowl, beat together the eggs, buttermilk, oil, and vanilla.

4. Gradually stir the wet ingredients into the dry ingredients.

5. Pour the boiling water into the batter and mix until combined.

6. Pour the batter into the prepared pan.

7. Bake in the preheated oven for 30 to 35 minutes, or until a toothpick inserted into the centre of the cake comes out clean.

8. Let cool before serving. Enjoy!

Banana Bread

Banana bread is a delicious and versatile dessert option that is sure to please any crowd. It is a classic comfort food that is easy to make and can be enjoyed as a snack, breakfast, or dessert. It is packed with flavour and nutrition, as it is made with whole wheat flour, ripe bananas, and other wholesome ingredients. Banana bread is a great way to use up overripe bananas and is a great way to satisfy a sweet tooth without overindulging. With its moist and fluffy texture and rich flavour, it is a crowd-pleasing dessert that is sure to be a hit with everyone!

Ingredients:

- 3 ripe bananas, mashed
- 1/3 cup melted butter
- 1 teaspoon baking soda
- Pinch of salt
- 3/4 cup sugar
- 1 large egg, beaten
- 1 teaspoon vanilla extract
- 1 1/2 cups all-purpose flour

Instructions:

1. Preheat the oven to 350°F (175°C). Grease a 9x5 inch loaf pan.

2. In a large bowl, mash bananas with a fork until almost smooth.

3. Stir melted butter into mashed bananas.

4. Mix baking soda and salt into the banana mixture.

5. Stir sugar, egg, and vanilla extract into the banana mixture.

6. Fold flour into the banana mixture until just blended.

7. Pour batter into the prepared loaf pan.

8. Bake in a preheated oven for 60 minutes, or until a toothpick inserted into the centre of the loaf comes out clean.

9. Let bread cool in a pan for 10 minutes, then turn out onto a wire rack. Cool completely before slicing.

4.3 Vegan Desserts

Vegan desserts are a great way to make a delicious treat without using animal products. Not only are vegan desserts a healthier alternative to traditional desserts, but they are also a great way to reduce your environmental footprint. Vegan desserts are made with plant-based ingredients such as fruits, nuts, and grains, which are much more sustainable than animal products. Furthermore, vegan desserts are often made without added sugar, making them a healthier choice for those with diabetes or other health conditions. Finally, vegan desserts are often dairy-free, making them a great option for those with lactose intolerance. With all these benefits, vegan desserts are a great way to enjoy a delicious treat without sacrificing your health or the environment.

Over the next few pages are some delicious vegan recipes to try:

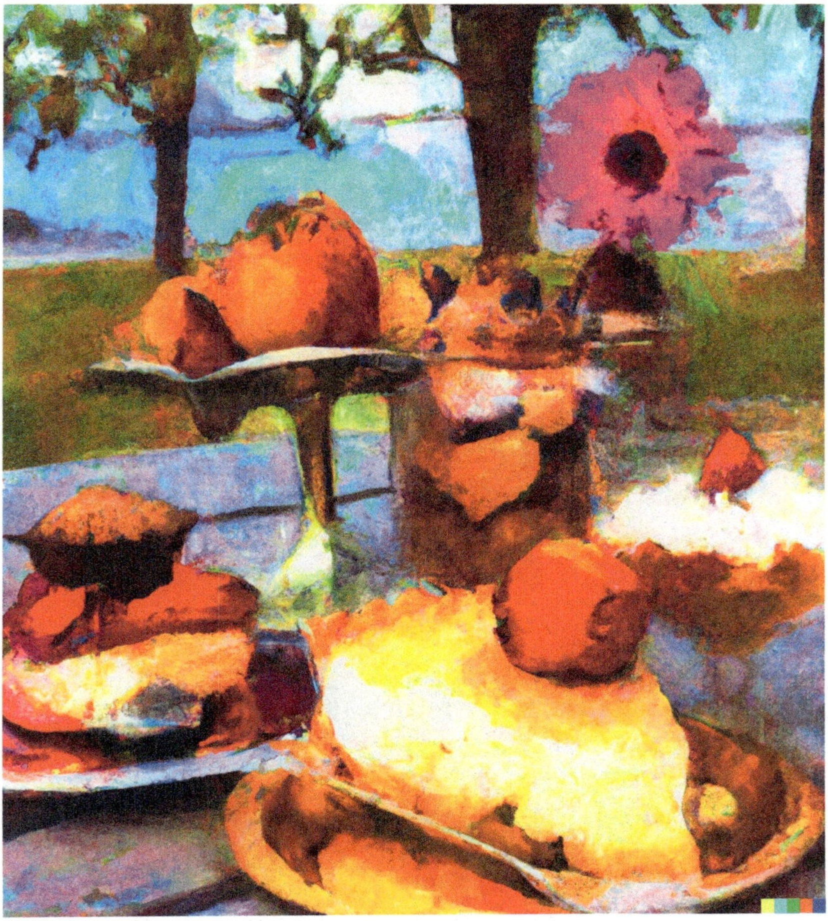

Chocolate Chip Cookies

Vegan Chocolate Chip Cookies are a great dessert option for those looking for a delicious treat that is also kind to animals and the environment. These cookies are made without any animal products, such as eggs, butter, or milk, making them a great choice for vegans and those with dietary restrictions. The chocolate chips add a delicious sweetness to the cookies, while the vegan ingredients make them a healthier alternative to traditional cookies. Vegan Chocolate Chip Cookies are a great way to satisfy your sweet tooth without compromising your values.

Ingredients:

- 2 1/4 cups all-purpose flour
- 1 teaspoon baking soda
- 1 teaspoon salt
- 1 cup (2 sticks) butter, softened
- 3/4 cup granulated sugar
- 3/4 cup packed brown sugar
- 1 teaspoon vanilla extract
- 2 large eggs
- 2 cups (12-oz. pkg.) semi-sweet chocolate chips
- 1 cup chopped nuts (optional)

Instructions:

1. Preheat the oven to 375°F.

2. Combine flour, baking soda and salt in a small bowl.

3. Beat butter, granulated sugar, brown sugar and vanilla extract in a large mixer bowl until creamy.

4. Add eggs, one at a time, beating well after each addition.

5. Gradually beat in flour mixture.

6. Stir in chocolate chips and nuts.

7. Drop by rounded tablespoon onto ungreased baking sheets.

8. Bake for 9 to 11 minutes or until golden brown.

9. Cool on baking sheets for 2 minutes; remove to wire racks to cool completely.

Banana Ice Cream

Vegan Banana Ice Cream is a delicious and healthy dessert option that is perfect for anyone looking to satisfy their sweet tooth without compromising their dietary restrictions. This vegan ice cream is made with only natural ingredients, such as bananas, coconut milk, and agave nectar, and is free of dairy, eggs, and other animal products. It is a great source of vitamins and minerals, and is also low in fat and calories. Plus, it is easy to make and can be customised with your favourite toppings. So if you're looking for a delicious and nutritious dessert, vegan banana ice cream is the perfect choice!

Ingredients:

- 3 ripe bananas
- 2 tablespoons of honey
- 2 tablespoons of peanut butter
- 1 teaspoon of vanilla extract
- 1/4 teaspoon of ground cinnamon
- 1/4 teaspoon of ground nutmeg
- 1/2 cup of heavy cream
- 1/2 cup of whole milk

Instructions:

1. Peel the bananas and place them in a blender.

2. Add the honey, peanut butter, vanilla extract, cinnamon, and nutmeg to the blender.

3. Blend the ingredients until smooth.

4. In a separate bowl, whisk together the heavy cream and milk until combined.

5. Slowly add the banana mixture to the cream and milk mixture, whisking until combined.

6. Pour the mixture into an ice cream maker and churn according to the manufacturer's instructions.

7. Once the ice cream is done churning, transfer it to a freezer-safe container and freeze for at least 4 hours before serving.

Carrot Cake

Vegan Carrot Cake is a delicious and healthy dessert option that is sure to please everyone. It is made with wholesome ingredients such as carrots, nuts, and spices, and is free of animal products such as eggs and dairy. This makes it a great choice for those who are vegan, or who are looking for a healthier alternative to traditional desserts. The moist and flavorful cake is also packed with vitamins and minerals, making it a great way to get your daily dose of nutrition. With its unique flavour and texture, vegan carrot cake is sure to be a hit at any gathering.

Ingredients:

- 2 cups all-purpose flour
- 2 teaspoons baking powder
- 1 teaspoon baking soda
- 1 teaspoon ground cinnamon
- 1/2 teaspoon ground nutmeg
- 1/4 teaspoon ground cloves
- 1/2 teaspoon salt
- 1 1/2 cups granulated sugar
- 1/2 cup vegetable oil
- 4 large eggs
- 2 teaspoons pure vanilla extract
- 2 cups finely grated carrots
- 1/2 cup chopped walnuts
- 1/2 cup raisins

Instructions:

1. Preheat the oven to 350°F (175°C). Grease and flour a 9x13 inch baking pan.

2. In a medium bowl, whisk together flour, baking powder, baking soda, cinnamon, nutmeg, cloves, and salt.

3. In a large bowl, beat together sugar, oil, eggs, and vanilla extract until light and creamy.

4. Gradually add the dry ingredients to the wet ingredients, stirring until just combined.

5. Fold in the carrots, walnuts, and raisins.

6. Pour the batter into the prepared pan and spread evenly.

7. Bake for 40-45 minutes, or until a toothpick inserted into the centre of the cake comes out clean.

8. Allow the cake to cool completely before serving. Enjoy!

Brownies

Vegan Brownies are a delicious and healthy dessert option for anyone looking to satisfy their sweet tooth without sacrificing their dietary preferences. They are made with plant-based ingredients such as cocoa powder, vegan butter, and plant-based milk, making them free from animal products. This makes them a great choice for vegans, vegetarians, and those with allergies or dietary restrictions. Furthermore, vegan brownies are incredibly delicious and can be enjoyed by all, regardless of dietary preference. They are also easy to make and can be customised with various ingredients to suit any taste. With all these benefits, vegan brownies are a great dessert option for any occasion.

Ingredients:

- 2/3 cup all-purpose flour
- 1/2 teaspoon baking powder
- 1/4 teaspoon salt
- 1/2 cup (1 stick) unsalted butter, melted
- 1 cup granulated sugar
- 2 large eggs
- 2 teaspoons vanilla extract
- 1/2 cup unsweetened cocoa powder
- 1/2 cup semi-sweet chocolate chips

Instructions:

1. Preheat the oven to 350°F.

2. Grease an 8-inch square baking pan and set aside.

3. In a medium bowl, whisk together the flour, baking powder, and salt.

4. In a large bowl, whisk together the melted butter and sugar until combined.

5. Add the eggs and vanilla and whisk until combined.

6. Add the cocoa powder and whisk until combined.

7. Add the dry ingredients and stir until just combined.

8. Fold in the chocolate chips.

9. Pour the batter into the prepared pan and spread evenly.

10. Bake for 25-30 minutes, or until a toothpick inserted in the centre comes out clean.

11. Let cool in the pan for 10 minutes before cutting into squares. Enjoy!

One last thing...

Cook with Chris offers a wide variety of recipes for all occasions and tastes. From healthy meals to quick dinners and delicious desserts, you'll find something to satisfy your cravings. So go ahead and explore the recipes and find something new to try. So don't wait any longer, grab your apron and get cooking! Enjoy the deliciousness that Cook with Chris has to offer.

Printed in Great Britain
by Amazon